YOU'VE GOT THAT *Spark*

Keys to Help You Win in Life

TYRUS J. HINTON

Copyright © 2023 by Tyrus J. Hinton.

All rights reserved.
No part of this book may be reproduced or used in any manner without written permission of the copyright owner except for the use of quotations in a book review.

Book Project Management:
Start Write | Raindrop Creative, INC.

Editors:
Gerald C. Simmons | Tiara Martin Brown | Jennifer Eiland

Book Cover/Creative Direction/Illustrations:
Rainah Davis

FIRST EDITION
ISBN: 978-0-998-7700-4-8
Raleigh, NC
www.tyrusjhinton.com

Unless otherwise noted, all Scripture references or quotations are from the New International Version of the Bible and marked NIV.

New International Version (NIV) Holy Bible, New International Version®, NIV® Copyright ©1973, 1978, 1984, 2011 by Biblica, Inc.® Used by permission. All rights reserved worldwide.

YOU'VE GOT THAT SPARK

TABLE OF CONTENTS

Introduction	7
Chapter 1: Your Individual Spark	25
Chapter 2: Chasing, Choosing & Continuing Love	51
Chapter 3: Starting, Growing, & Pivoting On Your Career Path	77
Chapter 4: Securing the Bag: Cultivating Your Business	91
Chapter 5: Creating Financial Security & A Legacy of Wealth	105
Conclusion	121

INTRODUCTION

Almost two years ago, I felt a strong urging from the Lord to produce a body of work on the subject of confidence. Well, as my Gen Z and Millennial kids would say, "Life be *'LIFE-ING,'*" and this book got away from me. However, I believe God's timing is genuinely his kindness towards us because I know this book is definitely needed now.

According to the *Apple Dictionary*, the word "confident" means:

> ***Feeling or showing certainty about something or in oneself.***

That same dictionary defines the word "confidence" as:

"The feeling or belief that one can rely on someone or something; firm trust; a feeling of self-assurance arising from one's appreciation of one's own abilities or qualities; and a feeling of self-assurance arising from one's appreciation of one's own abilities or qualities."

"Confident Confidence" demands that you dig deep within yourself. You can compare this experience to that of a pot of boiling water, in that, during your self-evaluation, whatever you are not confident about should come to the top so you can skim it off. As with boiling water, the water remains hot below the surface—where your true confidence lies. Whatever is "cooked" in this water will experience dramatic change. The heat, also known as your confidence, will stimulate additional self-assurance as you mature and learn to love yourself, despite shortcomings along the way.

Further self-examination reveals that confidence is based on competence and past experiences of success. *"Confident confidence"* is being assured of the inevitability of victory, *regardless* of past defeats. As Winston Churchill said, "Success is moving from failure to failure with no loss of enthusiasm." People who lack confidence say, "I don't think this will work." Confident people say, "I sure hope this works." People with "confident confidence" say, "This will work because I will *make* it work." This sentiment will be necessary as we end one season and head into the next.

The previous season was defined by COVID-19 and the domino effects that followed it. If we attempted to dive into all the ways our world was turned upside down during the pandemic, that would require a book of its own. Quarantines, civil unrest, vaccine debates, the housing crisis, remote work, and so many things changed our daily lives. As a bi-vocational pastor, I saw the pandemic's effects in the workplace and at our church. Neither the workforce nor the Christian community has fully rebounded from months of housebound necessity that shaped how we do things two years later. We are entering a new season marked by historic inflation and mass layoffs. Inflation can be felt in everything from major purchases like buying cars to weekly activities like buying eggs. *NPR* reported that in December 2022, the cost of eggs was up %60 over the previous year, according to the Consumer Price Index. If the sticker shock of inflation was not bad enough, people began losing their jobs left and right. According to Mondo, mass layoffs are defined this way:

- When at least 50 employees are laid off within 30-days or less, resulting in the laid-off employees equaling more than one-third of the company's workforce
- 500 employees are laid off within 30-days or less, no matter how large the company's workforce

As I pen the final words to this book, it is early February 2023. Within the first two months of quarter one, this is a partial list of mass layoffs of major corporations, also reported by Mondo (I have added the number of jobs for the companies who provided that information):

- **Disney layoffs:** *[7,000 jobs] 3% of the workforce laid off (February 2023)*
- **Zoom layoffs:** *[1,300 jobs] 15% of the workforce laid off (February 2023)*
- **Dell layoffs:** *[6,500 jobs] 5% of workforce laid off (February 2023)*
- **HubSpot layoffs:** *7% of workforce laid off (February 2023)*
- **PayPal layoffs:** *[2,000 jobs] 7% of workforce laid off (February 2023)*
- **IBM layoffs:** *[3,900 jobs] 1.5% of workforce laid off (January 2023)*
- **Gemini layoffs:** *10% of the workforce laid off (January 2023)*
- **Yankee Candle layoffs:** *13% of office workers laid off (January 2023)*
- **3M layoffs:** *<1% of workforce laid off (January 2023)*
- **Spotify layoffs:** *[400 jobs] 6% of workforce laid off (January 2023)*

- **Google (Alphabet) layoffs:** *[12,000 jobs] 6% of workforce laid off (January 2023)*
- **Microsoft layoffs:** *[10,000 jobs] 4-5% of the workforce laid off by the end of the first quarter (announced in January 2023)*
- **Amazon layoffs:** *1-2% of workforce laid off (January 2023)*
- **Carta layoffs:** *10% of workforce laid off (January 2023)*
- **Coinbase layoffs:** *20% of the workforce laid off (January 2023)*
- **DirecTV layoffs:** *5-6% of the workforce laid off (January 2023)*
- **Salesforce layoffs:** *[7,000 jobs] 10% of the workforce laid off (January 2023)*
- **Vimeo layoffs:** *11% of the workforce laid off (January 2023)*
- **Goldman Sachs layoffs:** *8% of workforce laid off (January 2023)*

This troubling development has caused me to shift my "confident confidence" mantra. People are tired, and they are scared. Confidence is only attainable by discovering and embracing inner giftings and natural inclinations. I'll give you an example.

I mentioned being a bi-vocational staff pastor. Well, my other job is in the property management field. I am a certified multi-family residential property manager. Recently, I had an interaction with a teacher who is transitioning into the property management industry. There was "a glow" my Gen Z kids would call "a vibe," and my Millennials (Gen Y) kids would call "good energy" about this young lady. I, a Gen Xer, couldn't help but label her personal as a "spark." She just had this spark about her. At that moment, I realized I needed to reconfigure this book to incorporate my newfound revelation. That revelation was that to survive and thrive in a spiraling economic downturn, people (you, me, all of us) needed to find the place where we come alive and get to work! For someone, that may require getting a certification; for someone else, that may include a degree; and for others, that may involve watching a few hours of YouTube videos. Whatever you have to do to get your spark to pop and sizzle, you need to get busy doing it, and I want to help you. So let's dig into my updated manifesto and the five keys that will help you win in life.

You've got that spark

There are treasures within us that we often don't look at as treasures, but in reality, they are a spark. Once a person has identified their spark, it builds their confidence. Once you determine what you're good at—that can be something as simple as talking to people or making them laugh—you've identified your spark. Sometimes it takes your spark to get your confidence rolling or to make you believe in yourself. I am here to inform you that you've got that spark, you've got that energy, you've got that fire, you've got, and it's already in you, but here are the layers and the levels to it. The groundwork we've done with "Confident Confidence" builds on what we're saying about that spark—that is the common theme.

With the workforce now spanning five generations, I must speak to people ages twenty to seventy. Whether you are just graduating from college or reinventing yourself to fight ageism, I want to help you find success faster.

Too many of us spend tens of thousands of dollars to go to school; listen, there is no judgment here. I have paid (and am still paying) almost $80,000 in college tuition. The issue is not school; it is when you have spent all that money and still need to figure out where you fit. My goal is to give you five Spark Keys to help you overcome labels, unfavorable pedigrees, imposter syndrome, and discouragement.

The Confidence Keys

Key #1 – The Spark Plug: Core Confidence

> spark plug | 'spärk ˌpləg | noun
> a device for firing the explosive mixture in an internal combustion engine.

Identifying Your Personal Calling

Core Confidence – This is an internal, individual confidence that allows you to flow freely and fluently in your gifts, calling, and passion. You are in trouble if your spark plugs stop working in your car. In the same way, you must ensure that this inner, personal confidence is working correctly because it unleashes you to give abundantly through philanthropic efforts, community outreach, or church service. It is difficult to pour from a place of emptiness, so we work on activating your complete inner confidence first. You cannot do any of this with a weak core. In physical training, core exercises are essential to a well-rounded fitness program. Your core is the central part of your body. It includes your pelvis, lower back, hips, and stomach. Core exercises train the muscles in your core to work in harmony. This regimen leads to better balance and steadiness, also called stability. In the same way, achieving core confidence provides the mental, spiritual, and physical equilibrium required to help you effortlessly execute your personal calling.

Key #2 – The Incense Spark

> in·cense | noun | ˈinˌsens | a gum, spice, or other substance that is burned for the sweet smell it produces: *the sharp lingering sweetness of incense [as modifier]: incense sticks.*
> the smoke or perfume of incense: *the swirls of incense in the air.*

Chasing, Choosing & Continuing Love

Couple Confidence – Over the last 15 years, I've had the privilege of counseling thousands of families and couples who are married, seeking marriage, divorced, intent to reconcile, separated, and just those who are thinking about committing themselves to one another. I even penned a book called Couples in Crisis to help fortify, strengthen, and save relationships from the issues that tragically tear people apart. I now endeavor to help couples in the embryonic stages of relationships. This key incorporates the use of "incense" because a good relationship has an aroma and an inviting scent. Additionally, incense sticks are a slow burn; they don't get lit fast, only to fizzle out even quicker. Instead of chasing and choosing love based on butterfly feelings and physical chemistry—I want to help to provide a new context for building a love that lasts. This premise is by establishing the couple has individual, complete confidence separately, and then they are equipped to come together and create a life that stands the test of time. That begins with our dating methods and leads to our marriage choice.

Key #3 – Firework Sparks

> Fire·work| ˈfī(ə)r,wərk | noun a device containing gunpowder and other combustible chemicals that causes a spectacular explosion when ignited, used typically for display or in celebrations
> | *[as modifier]: a firework display.*
> (**fireworks**) an outburst of emotion or a display of brilliance or energy

Starting, Growing, & Pivoting On Your Career Path

Career Confidence – Most people love fireworks. There is just something about lighting something that can light up the entire sky. That is what happens to you when you land the right career. Your brilliance is lit, and you light up the workplace. Your exuberant energy is on display for all to witness. Igniting the spark of career confidence can help you obtain your dream job. According to Study Finds, a survey of 2,000 Americans reveals that 43 percent are currently living out their childhood dream job, and an additional 19 percent have previously worked in their dream field. Many factors determine what people grow up wanting to be, their ability to follow that dream, and their ability to stay on that desired career path. Business Because reported, "The World Economic Forum estimates that by 2025, technology will create at least 12 million more jobs than it destroys. There will be a growing demand for data analysts and scientists, AI and machine learning specialists, and digital and marketing strategy specialists, among many more." This reality will force us to rethink and pivot some of our careers, and it will undoubtedly impact how will advise current and future generations. We will need to be more confident in our purpose and even more flexible in our work. The advancement of

AI technology will allow room for humans to focus on higher-value and higher-touch tasks requiring interpersonal interactions. Individuals will have more time to be creative, strategic, and entrepreneurial. These observations are the perfect segue into our next key.

Key #4 – The Campfire Spark

> camp·fire| 'kamp,fī(ə)r | noun an open-air fire in a camp, used for cooking and as a focal point for social activity:

Securing The Bag: Cultivating Your Business

    Commerce Confidence – 31 million people in the United States are entrepreneurs. According to the SBA (Small Business Association), small businesses have generated **12.9 million** net new jobs over the past 25 years, accounting for two out of every three jobs added to the economy. Worldwide, there are reported to be 582 million entrepreneurs. Approximately 55% of adults in the United States have owned a small business. All of these statistics are vital because most of these companies create jobs. This observation is significant because it makes what I call a "campfire spark," but not only does the business warm you, it can warm and benefit others. Please do not think I am forcing you to start your own business. There seems to be a massive push on social media to make everyone go out and create an LLC. Being an entrepreneur is not for the faint of heart.

Gregg Throgmartin, CEO of *Skin Laundry*, defines the term **entrepreneur** this way:

"...an entrepreneur is someone who can paint a vision of something that has never before existed, then work tirelessly to make it happen. Someone who lives and breathes their business, not because they have to, but because they love to. An entrepreneur is curious, passionate, and not afraid to dive headfirst into an area of opportunity where almost everyone else has failed before. They can either tune out the large chorus saying, "this won't work," or get fired up by the challenge to uncover and prove out just how it can work."

Does any part of this description describe you? If so, this is the easiest time in history to start your business; whether creating a side hustle to increase your income or establish a company—you need commerce confidence to bring your vision to pass. And it would help if you had this confidence key to stand fast while you are building. Because after you have created it, you will have new lists of wins and woes to celebrate and endure.

Key #5 – The Torch Spark

> torch | tôrCH | noun *mainly historical* a portable means of illumination such as a piece of wood or cloth soaked in tallow or an oil lamp on a pole sometimes carried ceremonially | (usually **the torch**) used to refer to a valuable quality, principle, or cause that needs to be protected and maintained.

Creating Financial Security & a Legacy of Wealth

Compound Coin Confidence: Before the Olympic Games opening, there is a torch-lighting ceremony. This ancient ritual is still in existence today. I want to propose that we begin to see legacy in that same way. Instead of defining financial security as only having a large savings account, a healthy investment portfolio, and a comfortable retirement nest egg, I endeavor to help you obtain financial freedom and legacy. In actuality, proper financial protection is about much more than just money. It's also about feeling in control of your life and having the freedom to choose how to live it. Compound coin confidence happens when you focus on legacy and plan for it regardless of your current circumstances.

My goal is to help you execute *at least one* of these keys in your life so that they provide benefit and value to you. I am excited to be your coach, mentor, and friend. Let's dive into this together!

CHAPTER 1
YOUR INDIVIDUAL SPARK

KEY #1 – THE SPARK PLUG: CORE CONFIDENCE

> spark plug | ˈspärk ˌpləg | noun
>   a device for firing the explosive mixture in an internal combustion engine.

Do you remember the first time a mechanic told you you needed spark plugs? If you are like me, you probably got mad and wondered if this was something made up to make you spend more money! Well, it turns out that was not the case. Spark plugs are vitally important to the life of your car. Spark plugs are an essential part of a car's engine and are necessary for several reasons:

1. Spark plugs provide the spark necessary to ignite the air/fuel mixture in the combustion chamber. Without this spark, the engine couldn't start or run.

2. Spark plugs are essential for the efficiency of the engine. They help burn the fuel more completely and quickly, which increases the power output of the engine and also helps to reduce emissions.
3. Spark plugs also help reduce wear and tear on other engine parts.

Burning fuel more efficiently reduces the amount of heat and force on other parts, which helps to prolong their lifespan.

Identifying Your Personal Calling

People are like spark plugs in the sense that they can provide a powerful burst of energy and ignite action when needed. Like a spark plug, people are essential components of a larger system and can make all the difference in how it functions. People can be reliable sources of energy, help to ignite ideas, and provide the spark that can propel a project or an organization to success. The first key we will discuss to ignite your inner spark is CORE CONFIDENCE. For the sake of this book, we define core confidence as internal, individual confidence that allows you to flow freely and fluently in your gifts, calling, and passion. If you are going to achieve this first level of confidence, you must strengthen your core. If you are wondering how to do it, don't worry. I am about to tell you right now.

Developing a Strong Core

One of the places that I visit frequently is Atlanta, Georgia. I create content there, visit family, and hang out with my friends. If you have ever been to the ATL airport, you most likely have taken a ride on the Plane Train to get you from one terminal to another. Inevitably, if significant time passes between visits, I sometimes forget how forceful the train is when it takes off! I am soon jolted, and I immediately remember I need to hold on to the straps, grab rails or grab bars – smaller handrails attached to seats, doors, and doorways. When this happened, I would either stumble forward or make a quick awkward motion to keep myself from crashing into a complete stranger. Yet, I have a friend who is a fitness trainer, and I noticed he never seemed to have that issue. I asked him one day what his Plane Train superpower was, and he laughed and said, "Tyrus, it's just core strength."

The answer seemed almost too simple to be accurate. However, as I mentioned in the introduction, a strong core trains your muscles to work in harmony, thus resulting in an overall internal strength that translates outwardly. Now that I regularly go to the gym, I, too, have developed this superpower. I am strong enough to shift my weight and plant my feet in a way that balances my body, even though the train is in motion.

Now, this chapter is not really about working out, even though a part of having core confidence is about being physically, mentally, and spiritually fit. And this trio is more about achieving your desired life than a number on a scale or your current BMI (body mass index).

This notion is crucial because there are nine factors to unlocking CORE CONFIDENCE. I will share them with you and then explain how I overcame obstacles to achieve this key factor in my life.

The nine factors involve unpacking and UNDERSTANDING SELF-ESTEEM. Before we dive in, it will be helpful to define it first.

Self-esteem refers to a person's overall sense of value or worth. It measures and evaluates how much a person "values, approves of, appreciates, prizes, or likes him or herself," according to authors Adler & Stewart (2004). Self-esteem expert Morris Rosenberg defines self-esteem as "simply one's attitude toward oneself" (1965). He also describes it as a "favorable or unfavorable attitude toward the self."

After reading an article by Positive Psychology, I had my team create a chart for you to see how many factors impact your self-esteem. I tweaked the list for better application.

I did not list them in any particular order. Still, I encourage you to take a journal and make notes about how each of these areas is presently impacting you or has impacted you in the past. You will see that the first factor listed is **age**. It is important to note how the components contribute to your overall self-esteem and self-worth. To achieve and maintain CORE confidence, you must study the makeup of your internal puzzle and unique wiring. I will briefly expound on each of these.

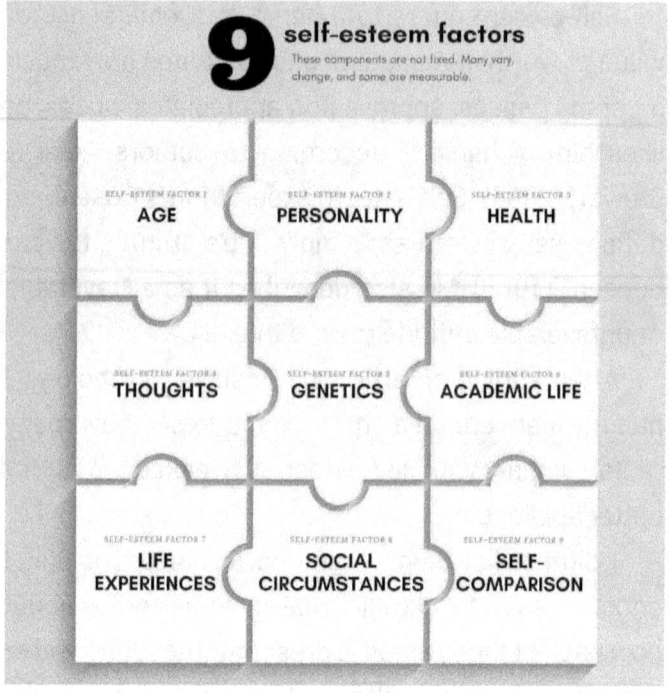

Age

Erik Erikson is a renowned American-German psychologist from the twentieth century. According to him, there are eight stages of life, which are defined as follows:

- Infancy
- Toddlerhood
- Preschool years
- Early school years
- Adolescence
- Young adulthood
- Middle adulthood
- Late adulthood

Whether you subscribe to his theories or agree with his philosophies, his life stages make it easier for us to relate our levels of esteem to a specific timeframe. Again, while I did not put these in any particular order, it is fitting that age begins our chart as infancy begins our lives.

Personality

Personality refers to a person's distinctive thinking, feeling, and behavior patterns. The American Psychological Association breaks it down further, "... the enduring characteristics and behavior that comprise a person's unique adjustment to life, including major traits, interests, drives, values, self-concept, abilities, and emotional patterns."

Traits and characteristics vary greatly, even within the same family. As a leader, manager, pastor, parent, or counselor, a personality test is one of the most helpful tools you can complete. There are many personality tests, but these are a few of the most popular.

- The Myers Briggs Type Indicator (MBTI) assigns individuals a psychological "type" summarized in four of eight possible letters: Extroversion (E) or Introversion (I); Sensing (S) or Intuiting (N); Thinking (T) or Feeling (F); and Judging (J) or Perceiving (P). The results combine into one of 16 types, such as ENTJ or ISFP. The MBTI is widely used in business—such as for employee evaluation or during seminars—and unofficial versions are available for personal use. However, scientists often cite its limitations, including that its separate "types" oversimplify personality differences.

- DISC or "DiSC" is the name given to a collection of personality assessments that assign individuals one of four types or a blend of the types: Dominance (D), Influence (I), Steadiness (S), and Conscientiousness (C). Like the Myers-Briggs, it is promoted for learning about individual personality differences within organizations. Still, it is generally not favored by contemporary personality scientists.
- Enneagram-related tests are based on the concept of the Enneagram of Personality and assign personality descriptions based on nine primary types and often secondary types called "wings." While the Enneagram has been promoted in business and spiritual contexts, it lacks empirical support and is infrequently used by personality scientists.

You will be surprised at how accurate the tests are when people answer the questions truthfully. It may not be 100 percent accurate to a tee, but typically they are close and provide tremendous insight.

Health

The functioning of your body is critical to your quality of life. It typically plays a crucial role in your self-esteem. Experts widely consider **exercise, good nutrition, relaxation, and sleep** essential to healthy living. While these so-called "four pillars" of good health help keep your body running, they also do wonders for your emotional well-being. The American Heart Association also lists practicing mindfulness, managing stress, keeping mind and body fit, and connecting socially equally essential components to developing and maintaining optimal health. These factors are crucial because they contribute to your external self. I cannot tell you how many people lack self-esteem because they do not like how they look. But those dissatisfied individuals struggle to succeed in one of the abovementioned areas. If these areas can be improved, self-esteem generally automatically increases. If you are looking for an excellent place to start, here are a few suggestions:

- Start by walking 30 minutes a day if you are physically able. If you are not, start by asking

your health provider for ways to get active safely.
- Eat healthier and try not to skip meals. You can start by eating more fruits and vegetables and eliminating fast and fried food. Remember, Rome was not built in the day. Start here.
- Get 6-8 hours of sleep and change your nighttime routine if you have trouble sleeping. The Sleep Foundation suggests "including calming activities like taking a warm bath, reading, journaling, or meditation" and eliminating electronics before bedtime.

Thoughts

While these are in no particular order, health and thoughts are strongly connected. The University of Minnesota defines thoughts this way, "thoughts are mental cognitions—our ideas, opinions, and beliefs about ourselves and the world around us. They include the perspectives we bring to any situation or experience that color our point of view (for better, worse, or neutral)."

This factor is so critical I want to go in-depth regarding my development in achieving CORE CONFIDENCE.

I've struggled with confidence (or a lack thereof) for as long as I can remember. My low self-esteem started at home. Growing up, I distinctly remember my dad telling me multiple times, "You're my number-one dumb son! You're stupid, just like your mother! You don't know anything!" Those were his words to me verbatim, and "put down" was the language hurled toward me until I was about sixteen. His words began to play on repeat in my head and became the soundtrack of thoughts that cycled daily, like a favorite song left on repeat in a playlist. His words dominated my thought life.

Despite my father's negative feedback, intelligence *was* in me; the ability to produce *was* in me. Confidence was the missing link. I needed it to have a clear differentiator factor between success and failure for me. That experience taught me that if someone can strip somebody's confidence early enough, they can keep them in a hole of debasement for the rest of their lives. If someone can make someone else feel that they are not adequate and will never measure up to the world's expectations, then eventually, they will slavishly adhere to those lies.

I thank God that my situation turned out differently. I thank Him for my grandmother, who always told me she loved and taught me about Jesus. I thank the Lord for my teachers who taught me the joys of learning. Over time, God orchestrated my steps and gave me confidence at home and school. I might not have been as good as everybody else; still, I began believing in my talents and ability to improve. If you are going to change your life, you first have to change your thoughts. This factor is one of the reasons I am a believer in affirmations. Sometimes before you can think differently, you have to say something different. I pray that you and every one person connected to you will get free from negative thinking and be delivered from the negative words spoken over you through every stage of your life.

Genetics

The National Institute of General Medical Sciences (NIGMI) defines genetics as the scientific study of genes and heredity—how certain qualities or traits are passed from parents to offspring. The definition of genetics is not as important as how you use the information. Moreover, it is equally important not to let the limitations of your family prevent you from embracing your CORE CONFIDENCE. In the THOUGHTS section, I started sharing about my dad. Since he wasn't present at home much, I tried not to let his words affect me. However, he ensured I knew my brother was his favorite when he came around.

Consequently, I resented my half-brother because my dad loved his mother more than he loved mine and loved him more than he loved me. My biological mother had a substance abuse problem. Because of her challenges, when I was born, I was placed into a foster care program for the first three months of my life. My father promised my mother never to see me again to get me out of that system. She agreed, and under this condition, my dad removed me from foster care.

Therefore, under these unfortunate circumstances, my lack of confidence began. To my paternal grandmother's credit, she did her best to affirm me, but I missed my biological mom. I desired an authentic mother-son relationship, mainly because I did not get along with my dad. Overall, I lacked a strong support system in my youth and could not believe in myself. It would have been easy to allow my rough entry into the world to limit me. And I may even be justified by some if I let my mother's addiction and abandonment entirely shape my life and prevent me from seeking confidence and success. But I refused to do that. It became the opposite for me. I am determined to be a good father, as tough as that can be in today's world. I am determined to encourage my kids, even when they drive me nuts. I refuse to let anyone love my family better than me. I want you to take your genetics and do a personal evaluation. You may wonder, "Tyrus, how in the world will I do that?" Well, I am so glad you asked.

I want you to take the **SWOTS** approach to integrate this knowledge into your life. For those unfamiliar, **SWOTS is an acronym for STRENGTHS, WEAKNESSES, OPPORTUNITIES, THREATS, and STRATEGIES**. Some people stop at the **T**, but I am a solution-oriented individual and want you also to take this approach. You need to apply these five criteria to your genetic makeup and background. I gave you a head start on questions you need to ask yourself, your parents, siblings, or other family members. The answers can help you create a plan of action to continue doing good things in your lineage and destroy the faulty characteristics and behaviors in your family tree.

- **Strengths** – What are my parents naturally good at doing? Siblings? Other family members?
- **Weaknesses** – In what areas do my parents struggle? What are the major character flaws I can honestly observe in my family? What generational curses need to be broken?

- **Opportunities** – How can I be the game changer? How can I be a chain breaker for deficiencies in my bloodline? How can I flip the script and be the first millionaire, the first college graduate, the first person to be married to one person, or even the first person to have children by the same person? If I have already made a bunch of mistakes, how can I raise my children to seek these opportunities? Who can I mentor if I have made these mistakes and have no children? Who can I help?
- **Threats** – What challenges am I prone to face based on my lineage? What diseases have we seen for multiple generations? Asking these questions is an excellent way to think through some of the opposition you will have to fight to overcome.
- **Strategies** – What do I need to do differently to achieve a different result than generations before me?

Academic Life

I started sharing details of my early life in the thoughts section. I mentioned the negativity of my father. Due to my dad's lack of education, he had low self-esteem and a bad attitude. His negativity paralyzed me academically. I struggled until I began high school but encountered teachers willing to help me. They could identify that I could do my assignments, but I wasn't confident in my ability. What is more, my lack of confidence directly affected my output.

For years, I allowed my dad's demeaning viewpoint to hinder me from putting forth my best foot forward, for I had truly believed that I was Dad's *"number-one dumb son."* I embraced that label because that's who my dad said I was; moreover, I engaged in silly and stupid behavior because I thought that this conduct was all that I could do. Yet these stigmatizing tirades were lies. Gently and professionally, my teachers showed me how to understand better what I was reading. Additionally, I soon learned that I could relate to numbers and that arithmetic was easy. I developed an appreciation for geography and American history that I had never had before. Miraculously, high school became a safe place because my teachers gave me the push I needed to accomplish more extraordinary things. If you have struggled to achieve educational success, I want to stop and tell you to go for it. College is undoubtedly waning in popularity (primarily due to costs). Don't let the financial aspect deter you; many grants are available, especially for bachelor's degrees. If you never graduated from high school, I urge you to get your GED and keep going. Online courses are available now if you learn better via video and have difficulty in traditional classroom settings. One platform that I have heard positive reviews about is COURSEA. Google also has free classes. And Youtube is another educational resource. It is now considered a search engine for information more than an entertainment platform. You will be surprised at the level your CORE confidence rises with academic achievement, regardless of the type. Whatever you are good at, I challenge you to learn more about it this year. It is a confident confidence booster!

Life Experiences

I have friends and colleagues from all walks of life. Yet, in my experiences, as an African American male, racism and discrimination are two significant adverse effects on self-esteem that I have had to overcome. These are two factors that create unique life experiences. As a result, in management roles, I work hard to eliminate all discrimination and bias so that toxic workplace effects are eliminated or at least minimized. Many years ago, I decided to advocate for safe and healthy office environments because workplace traumas create horrific experiences that can harm people for years.

As a counselor, I often see individuals' life experiences shatter their self-esteem. For example, low self-esteem might be caused by overly critical or negative assessments from family and friends. Your life experiences matter and I encourage you to take steps to heal. For some of you, that will mean you need therapy; for others, that may mean changing your environment and inner circle. Whatever it means for you, I encourage you to intentionally heal from past harmful life experiences and choose better surroundings for better future outcomes.

Social Circumstances

There are pros and cons to being born wealthy, middle-class, and low-income. No one is exempt from challenges, and your social standing just dictates what type of challenges you have. I have friends from affluent families, and the upside for them is that they often do not experience financial hardship. Still, they do struggle relationally because they question people's motives. People with means are more likely to wonder if people are in a relationship with them for their wealth or because they are genuinely attracted to them. This factor can make authentic relationships difficult for them to obtain and maintain.

Individuals born in middle-class families can suffer from being in the middle. These people are not wealthy enough to be considered rich but have too much to be considered poor. Unfortunately, this can create awkward social situations for them. While this group fits in with one another, they can be ostracized by the other two groups (wealthy and low-income).

People from low-income backgrounds struggle with economic mobility. Still, they often have more tight-knit family structures because all they have is each other. There tends to be a great emphasis on family. Also, these family members tend to do more together because of fewer resources. I have a friend who was raised by a single mom, and they walked almost everywhere because they did not have a car until he was 15. Now, this would not be a big deal to many of us raised in the northern United States, but in the south...trust me, you need a vehicle to get around!

Everyone's situations are different; these are just a few observations from people I know. Within culture groups, other factors create unique social circumstances. For people of color, colorism is real. Individuals are treated differently based on the hue of their complexion. Living in the suburbs versus public housing creates vastly different social experiences for urban populations. My Caucasian colleagues share stories of ill-treatment within their families between family members who live in mansion-like houses versus family members living in tenements or trailer parks – depending on the region. Many factors shape your social experiences, which greatly influence your self-esteem.

Self-Comparison

Today self-comparison can be best summarized by understanding the social comparison theory. According to *Psychology Today*, social comparison theory is the idea that individuals determine their own social and personal worth based on how they stack up against others. The theory was developed in 1954 by psychologist Leon Festinger. The same article reports that as much as 10 percent of our thoughts involve comparisons of some kind, specifically concerning domains like attractiveness, wealth, intelligence, and success.

Does this strike a chord with you? Are you guilty of looking to others to affirm your self-assurance? In the past, I know I have. My father favored my brother, failed to support me the way I needed, and made me feel unworthy of love. At my breaking point, while I could've begun to compare how I was better than my brother, I chose a different route. I decided to start applying myself more in school and stop depending on my dad for praise or direction; that deliberate turnaround was when things began to turn around for me. My spark was ignited as I let go of the negative factors gripping me tightly. Doing so enabled God to use my dysfunctional household to push me toward greatness. Instead of submitting to the toxicity that my father was spewing and making me believe that I was less than my brother, I decided to use my hardships as motivation and consequently begin to make self-improvements.

Can you recall a time when comparison worked to your advantage? Maybe a coach thought your teammate was destined to outperform you, but you proved both the coach and teammate wrong during a game. What happened? Now, consider what the pros of your situation were.

On the contrary, perhaps you are familiar with the misconceptions about the concept of comparison. Some of these thoughts include the following:

1. Comparison is a killer
2. Comparison is a thief of joy
3. Comparison lacks contentment

Furthermore, comparing can be toxic if you constantly put yourself down and are not secure in your identity. However, comparing can be healthy and motivational if you like who you are and aspire to grow, for the expansion of your mind and thoughts is an expansion of you. When you learn to compare your strengths and weaknesses daringly, you can overcome your challenges and enhance your strengths. I want you to practice self-comparison to bring about positive, healthy change in your life and light up your spark plug of **core confidence**!

CHAPTER 2
CHASING, CHOOSING & CONTINUING LOVE

KEY#2 – THE INCENSE SPARK

in·cense | noun | 'in,sens | a gum, spice, or other substance that is burned for the sweet smell it produces: *the sharp lingering sweetness of incense [as modifier]: incense sticks.* • the smoke or perfume of incense: *the swirls of incense in the air.*

Couple Confidence

Over the last 15 years, I've had the privilege of counseling thousands of families and couples who are married, seeking marriage, divorced, intent to reconcile, separated, and just those who are thinking about committing themselves to one another. I even penned a book called Couples in Crisis to help fortify, strengthen, and save relationships from the issues that tragically tear people apart. I now endeavor to help couples in the embryonic stages of relationships. This key incorporates the use of "incense" because a good relationship has an aroma and an inviting scent. Additionally, incense sticks are a slow burn; they don't get lit fast, only to fizzle out even quicker. Instead of chasing and choosing love based on butterfly feelings and physical chemistry—I want to help to provide a new context for building a love that lasts. This premise is by establishing the couple has individual, complete confidence separately. Then they are equipped to come together and create a life that stands the test of time. That begins with our dating methods and leads to our marriage choice.

Matthew 7:24-27 New International Version
The Wise and Foolish Builders

> *24 "Therefore, everyone who hears these words of mine and puts them into practice is like a wise man who built his house on the rock. 25 The rain came down, the streams rose, and the winds blew and beat against that house, yet it did not fall because it had its foundation on the rock. 26 But everyone who*

> *hears these words of mine and does not put them into practice is like a foolish man who built his house on sand. **27** The rain came down, the streams rose, and the winds blew and beat against that house, and it fell with a great crash."*

I mentioned to you all that I am a pastor. One of the facets of that vocation is using biblical truths to improve daily life with practical, real-life application. The parable in Matthew Chapter 7 illustrates the importance of building a solid foundation. The most vital element to building on a firm foundation is where you build. In this story, Jesus explains the devastating effects of being a foolish builder. And you and I do not want to build a house that will come crashing down! So, we must be intentional about where and who is building with us. I have learned that the quality of your life is based on good decisions and two decisions more than any other. First, as a believer −I believe that my Christian faith is paramount to the quality of life that I enjoy. Next, almost equally, is the wife of my youth, that I have been rocking with for nearly three decades. These two decisions—becoming a believer and choosing the right partner have significantly shaped my life for the better. If you have relationship questions or issues or want more on this topic, I wrote an entire book called Couples in Crisis. It is helpful to both work your way out of an ongoing crisis, and it also provides tools for crisis prevention. Again, I know how tough relationships can be because I have been married to the same woman without separation for over 25 years. And in modern times, when blended families are even more popular, relationships can be even more challenging. I want to give you a little of our background that will lay some necessary groundwork for COUPLE CONFIDENCE.

I was pretty young when I started dating my wife. In fact, we were high school students attending two separate schools. Back in the day, the older generations used to call it "puppy love." My mom repeatedly told me that I had no clue what love was! She often reminded me that my real focus should be on my studies and not to worry because I would know when the right one came along. Now, to be clear, it is not that my mom didn't care for my girlfriend; she was just concerned about anything that would divert my attention from my schoolwork since I often struggled with maintaining above-average grades.

Reminiscing, I distinctly recall how different our families were. Her mom was very spiritual, private, quiet, structured, and routined. She maintained a very serious demeanor. She didn't play any games. Looking back, I considered it a major breakthrough when she began to like me. She realized I was a religious, respectable, well-mannered, neatly dressed young man who treated her daughter with respect. She welcomed me to visit her home (with her present, of course) as often as I liked after school and on the weekends. Behind all of that goodness remained our biggest difference; my girlfriend (her daughter) was an honors student who was very disciplined in her studies, and I was the polar opposite.

My mom was similar; quiet, spiritual, structured, routine, and was not to be played with either. My mom often said, "You play with toys, not me!" While our mothers had the same core values, our families were different. We constantly hosted big family gatherings. We were loud and over the top with everything. Every time we came together, it was like a holiday of sorts. There were always multiple conversations happening, which caused an insanely high noise level. We had enormous gatherings with everyone present. We had aunts, uncles, sisters, brothers, cousins, play cousins, neighborhood friends, family members, co-workers, church members, and sometimes their friends and family. Our house would get packed quickly. Now on my girlfriend's side, they were very private and quiet. Never a crowded or loud home. They knew name by name who was in the house at all times.

Additionally, she was raised by her mom, while I was raised by my paternal grandmother. This factor resulted in our upbringings varying vastly in both age and views.

Talk about a challenge!

Fast forward, we dated our last three years of high school and first year of college. Around this time, we experienced our first family crisis. My family began to have an issue with the time, energy, and effort I put into my relationship. My family started to pressure me to spend more time with them. They became upset when I chose to be with my girlfriend rather than attend a family gathering. These situations began to erode our "couple confidence." The negativity could have extinguished the spark of the sweet-smelling incense we had come to enjoy as a couple.

Outside forces will often be the greatest saboteur of relationship foundations.

At this point, I had to determine whether to defend my girlfriend and our relationship or I would allow my family to treat me as if I was still everyone's favorite little boy. I was the "Golden Child." I learned a valuable lesson during that period of my life.

Our relationship began to experience some very intense difficulty because of my inability to defend our relationship with confidence. Based on my family's history of dysfunctional romantic relationships, our family had a very negative, selfish view and approach to having any relationship with someone outside the home. As far as my family was concerned, the other person is **temporary**, but we are your family **forever**.

Looking back, I realize that my family did a fantastic job preparing us for college, careers, and financial success, but there was almost an inability to truly let the eaglets out of the nest and fly. It was as if my family never imagined or considered that, at some point, I would "leave and cleave" to my wife. At that time, they couldn't see her as a wife; she was just my girlfriend. I had to remind my family that they had prepared me for life and love in the future. I do not believe they disagreed with me in theory. The truth was that they just hadn't set a realistic timeframe for what my manhood would mean for the future. So, in selfishness, they began to make statements and plant negative seeds that would cause me to look at my girlfriend differently and sometimes even slightly change a little. It's not that I was weak-minded; it was just up until that point in my life my family's voices were the ones that resonated with me the most because I had been listening to them regarding every major decision my entire life.

The situation worsened as my actions and words differed, and the strain on our relationship was almost unbearable. Because of family, we went days without speaking (which is very unhealthy when building relationships). The truth is selfishness will never work when building relationships. Well, thank goodness, we had a few seasoned couples around us who had been married for a few years, providing little insight into what was happening with us. They offered the intervention we needed to put our relationship back on the right track. While this is true in some aspects, in developing relationships, we cannot afford to see the person we are building with as temporary. When our view of the person we are with is long-term, we can defend our decision with confidence and clarity.

When the relationship is fueled with couple confidence, it is not only a blessing to the couple but to everyone connected to them. A good marriage gives off a beautiful, alluring aroma. That is why I call it the "incense spark."

In many religious practices, burning incense is believed to **deepen our attention and empower our**

spiritual focus. The aroma of incense can help you tap into your spiritual connections. It calms the environment and your mind, cleansing the space for inner and outer journeys.

Incense Benefits

- Increase calm and focus
- Stress and anxiety reduction
- Improved rest and sleep
- Stimulate your creativity
- Purify your space
- Total environmental enhancement

Think about it; healthy relationships have the same or at least similar benefits. You can use the benefits above to create a Couple Confidence Blueprint for your relationship.

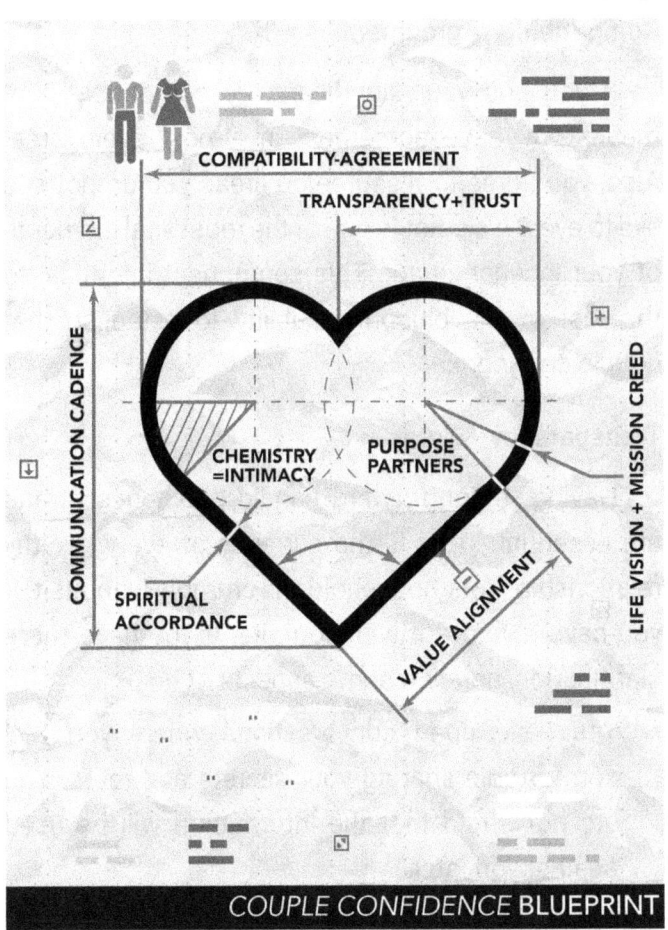

Couple Confidence Blueprint Components:

Compatibility-Agreement

If you and your significant are compatible, that means you have agreement in almost every area. Also, you agree to disagree on areas you do not see eye to eye. This point is one of the most vital elements of your incense spark. This component is critical to the rest of the blueprint's ability to establish true couple confidence.

Transparency + Trust

Having straightforward, candid, and honesty traits are essential. Trust is the currency of every healthy relationship. Your household will crumble without it. If you have it, guard it with your life. If you need more clarification, here are some aspects of it.

- You have open conversations where you feel comfortable sharing your secrets and fears. You are not afraid that the information will be used against you later.
- You maintain good non-verbal body language; for example, you look your partner in the eyes showing

you have nothing to hide. You can do this even during times of conflict.
- You are an active listener. You do not only listen to reply; you listen to retain the information shared by your loved one.
- You have a healthy conflict with favorable resolutions. This interaction looks like readily admitting mistakes, forgiving quickly, and not holding grudges.
- You take accountability for areas where you need to mature, grow, or change instead of making excuses.
- Your relationship is an intimate friendship with love, laughter, and care.

Communication Cadence

In healthy relationships, there is a rhythm and flow to conversations and verbal interactions. I like to think of it as a communication cadence, just like a drum line creates a melody with a specific beat. Orchestras create beautiful harmonic pieces, with every instrument playing its section of the music. Playing well together is required for well-executed concerts; couples must flow together to maintain a Couple Confidence blueprint. Sheet music is an excellent example of how this works. In some parts, different sections of instruments may be playing while others are at rest.

In the same way, how we converse when we talk to one other; and what we say is critical if our communication will have a harmonious melody. This level of alignment is often created by adopting a wholesome, calm, friendly, and patient communication style. When this happens, the offense is not quickly taken, and both assume the other's motives are unintentional— even on the rare occasions when their tone shows signs of agitation, moodiness, or aggression. This truth means we must fight not to let our emotions disrupt the cadence of our communication.

Spiritual Accordance

This one is straightforward to explain but complex to practice. It means a couple believes the same thing or respects each other's differing belief systems. To adopt and maintain couple confidence, you need to feel good about the spiritual leanings of your partner. If you two agree to practice different faiths, you must quickly decide what religion your future children (or bonus children) will participate in and practice. I have seen many couples unravel at the contention over faith practices. The reason this occurs is because of holiday observances and principles that may vary from one religion to another. Another challenge that can surface is whether one person is agnostic or atheist. Whatever your beliefs are, it is critical for you two to be on one accord as it relates to faith application and observance.

Purpose Partners: In long-term relationships, it is critical to accept that you either grow together, or you grow apart. If you are going to grow together, you must become purpose partners. If you are wondering, "Tyrus, are you saying I need to be with someone who has the same purpose as me?"

I would answer, "Absolutely not."

However, you do need to link your purposes together and forge a partnership. This partnership includes a value alignment of your core values and a joint life vision + mission creed. These two elements are also a part of the Couple Confidence blueprint. First, you must be clear on your purpose, so you know how your partnership will function. Because sometimes, the partnership looks like cheering on your spouse in their respective field; other times, it could be advising them if you have a skill set that they could benefit from utilizing in their career. For example, a dance studio owner may have a significant other that is a photographer. The photographer could enhance the studio owner's marketing, media, and visual capacity by operating in their gift. And suppose you and your spouse's vocations have nothing to do with one another. In that case, that is okay because occupation and purpose are not the same. Your purpose is what you are uniquely called to do in the Earth. So the key is supporting your partner in their calling. After giving support, the key is to see how to take your purposes (individual) and continue to grow together. Again, we discuss this more in two of the other components.

Chemistry = Intimacy

I will not spend much time on this section because we are all grown. Yet, I cannot assume that you know. You need to be attracted to the person you are going to spend the rest of your life hugging, kissing, and sexing. Yes, looks will fade, but they don't fade that fast! I cannot tell you how many couples are in trouble because someone told them that looks don't matter. After counseling for almost three decades, I can tell you that it is rare that couples who are not attracted to each other or have no chemistry are happy long-term. Most are not content or satisfied short term because attraction, chemistry, and intimacy are critical to a monogamous, long-lasting, loving, and enjoyable relationship. One of the top issues I see in marriage therapy is men whose wives don't sleep with their husbands because they don't enjoy it or are not attracted to the man. With men, unless the guy is just a dog, they typically want to be with their wives, but if they are not clean, shaven (for some), or not "into" them, it will make them desire someone else. And before the ladies get me, hygiene is an issue on both sides of the tables. Women ask me if I can ask their men to take a shower before starting foreplay, so in addition to the attraction factor, we do need to make sure our bodies are in a condition that is pleasing to our mates. We also need to be emotionally available instead of just wishing to sleep with our partners.

Other challenges involve people who are either physically a rotten match or have different libidos; one lacks the desire to satiate the other or is restrained by a taboo that they deem impossible to overcome. All in all, we need to take the time to learn our partner's preferences because it is never good to assume. Intimacy should be a joyful adventure. And if you are dating someone, I recommend you have these conversations as soon as it looks like they are the "one." *Quick PSA: If either of you has been a victim of sexual abuse, seek counseling as soon as you can.*

Often, abuse can be buried so deep that it is tough to communicate. You owe it to yourself and your partner to talk through your pain to truly experience the pleasure you both long for and deserve.

Value Alignment

Working with Millennials and Gen Z has made me hypersensitive to generations who want to work somewhere that aligns with their core values. The more I see this, the more I realize that all the couples that I know who have good relationships have the same or at least similar core values. These values represent comparable fundamental beliefs and norms of behavior. The difference between right and wrong, or acceptable and unacceptable, is understood mainly by both without explanation. I love the definition provided by *Psychology Today*:

Core values in a relationship are the guiding beliefs that direct your words and actions; your perspective is about yourself, others, and the world around you. Core values are the foundation of how you live your life.

Here are some examples of important, common core values:

- Trustworthiness
- Family first
- Accountability
- Anger management or expression
- Empathy or emotional intelligence
- Self-improvement and awareness
- Loyalty
- Dependability
- Integrity
- Generosity
- Courage
- Gratitude
- Sustainability
- Self-respect
- Adaptability
- Uniqueness
- Assertiveness
- Support
- Open-mindedness
- Personal growth

- Flexibility
- Frugality or financial responsibility
- Self-reliance
- Soul Care and Self-care/Well-being

I want to give you a relational cheat code: your top five or ten should match or align with anyone you are doing life with long-term that is true in romance, career, and business. We will tackle that more in upcoming chapters.

Life Vision + Mission Creed

I am unsure if your family has a family crest, but if you do, I applaud you. I believe every couple and family should have a crest. Still, more importantly, everyone should be aware of what the crests represent. It should start with what your family does or will do on the earth. What does the family stand for, and how is that expressed? If your family is serious about empowering humanity, what vehicles are being used to accomplish that goal? Is the goal met through education, ministry, and philanthropy? If you have never thought about it, I suggest you do, especially if you have not had kids yet. But whether children are in your future or not, you should have your own goals, objectives, mission, and vision as a couple.

In the book *Leadership: A Communication Perspective* by Michael Hackman & Craig E. Johnson lists five characteristics of transformational leaders, those are:

- Creative (innovative)
- Interactive (masterful communicators able to articulate complex concepts clearly)
- Visionary (capable of delivering compelling, desirable, and attainable vision)
- Empowering (efficient in encouraging participation and involvement)
- Passionate (love the people they serve with and the work that they do with unmatched enthusiasm)

I believe that couples who develop and practice a personal life vision + mission creed function as the transformational leaders of their household. And they start or revise their lives by thinking about the end proactively. We will discuss legacy in later chapters, but for now, I want to introduce this concept to you from the lens of a relationship because we are better together. And if you are single, instead of just looking at her hips or his biceps, I want you to decide if you can create a life mission with that person. You will obtain a different level of confidence. Your relationship will emit a beautiful fragrance when it is built on a solid foundation by wise builders. Complete the exercise to get started.

Life Vision & Mission Creed Exercise

First, create a vision creed for your relationship, which is similar to a vision statement. The best vision statements provide a sense of direction and project an idea or image of a desirable future. They are comprised of the core values of both partners. Use the list above to identify your core values.

Develop a vision statement by combining your terminal values (lifelong goals) with your instrumental goals (behaviors that help others achieve lifelong goals). There are samples provided for each; there are spaces for you to add more.

Terminal Values

Mutual submission (we submit to one another based on skill/ability/experience/expertise)
Wisdom (practical understanding)
Joy (contentment)
Covenant (mutual committed love)

_____
_____
_____
_____

Instrumental Values

Consistency (competent, effective)
Honest (truthful, sincere)
Bravery (courageous)
Innovative (creative, imaginative, game-changing)
Loving (affectionate)

_____
_____
_____
_____
_____

Tyrus J. Hinton

Write yours here:

CHAPTER 3
STARTING, GROWING, & PIVOTING ON YOUR CAREER PATH

KEY #3 – FIREWORK SPARKS

> fire·work| ˈfī(ə)rˌwərk | noun a device containing gunpowder and other combustible chemicals that causes a spectacular explosion when ignited, used typically for display or in celebrations *[as modifier]: a firework display.*
> (**fireworks**) an outburst of emotion or a display of brilliance or energy.

Career Confidence

Most people love fireworks. There is just something about lighting something that can light up the entire sky. That is what happens to you when you land the right career. Your brilliance is lit, and you light up the workplace. Your exuberant energy is on display for all to witness. Igniting the spark of career confidence can help you obtain your dream job. According to Study Finds, a survey of 2,000 Americans reveals that forty-three percent are currently living out their childhood dream job, and an additional nineteen percent have previously worked in their dream field. Many factors determine what people grow up wanting to be, their ability to follow that dream, and their ability to stay on that desired career path. This section is for those who are new to their chosen career. Still, these same steps can be applied to a growing segment of the population (young and old) who are navigating a career pivot. *Inc* reported: "Career pivoting has become more common among professionals, especially during times of uncertainty, profound changes, and increased burnout." Knowing what makes a successful career pivot is essential to continued career growth, even if that growth puts you in a new industry.

While a career change can be daunting because it could mean starting over, people are still choosing to switch." There are many other reasons you should be intentional in your career pivots. The Great Resignation after COVID-19 prompted many individuals to take this leap. You must execute the shift well because it is critical to do it without burning bridges, if possible, even for a good reason. According to Pew Research, the majority of workers who quit a job in 2021 say low pay (63%), no opportunities for advancement (63%), and feeling disrespected at work (57%) were reasons why they quit, according to the Feb. 7-13, 2021 survey. At least one-third said that these were a *significant* reason for leaving.

Additionally, roughly half say that childcare issues were one reason why they quit a job (48% among those with a child younger than 18 in the household). Many others noted a need for more flexibility in choosing when they put in their hours (45%) or not having good benefits such as health insurance and paid time off (43%). Roughly a quarter say each of these was a *significant* reason; all these instances contributed to the surge of people who quit their jobs during the Great Resignation. While researching for this book, I read an article on *Inc*. A *Quora* contributor made some meaningful points I want to share with you. First, a career pivot can mean many different things in the workplace. Here are some examples:

- Working on different projects
- Switching work group or team
- Quitting
- Completely switching careers
- Asking for a promotion to a position you believe is more suitable to your ability

Next, the reasons for pivoting can also vary:

- Bad boss
- Co-workers who conspire against you
- Mind-numbingly dull work that feels pointless
- Working for a company that you think is going in the wrong direction
- Yearning to make much more money than you currently do
- Being forced to return to in-person office work

Understanding pivots and executing your career change effectively is essential because the world is changing. AI is an excellent example of that. *Business Because* reported, "The World Economic Forum estimates that by 2025, technology will create at least twelve million more jobs than it destroys. There will be a growing demand for data analysts and scientists, AI and machine learning specialists, and digital and marketing strategy specialists, among many more." This reality will force us to rethink and pivot some of our careers, undoubtedly impacting how we advise current and future generations. We must be more confident in our purpose and even more flexible in our work. These observations are the perfect segue into our next key.

We live in a fascinating time where people constantly put out the deepest, most intimate details about themselves on social media for the world to see. People who overshare, in a sense, seem strangely frustrated and even enraged when that same information (that they shared) is used against them negatively. This trend has become particularly troubling to me as a father of young adults. I cannot emphasize enough that everyone does not need to know everything about you, your life, and your struggles.

There is one person, however, who does need to know all of that—the good, the bad, and the ugly—that person is you. In addition to identifying and accepting the "real" you, you also have to be committed to fixing what needs to be fixed and loving the "real" you. Earlier in the book, we mentioned SWOT for your genetic profile. I want to discuss the "S" and "W" again here because it is vital if you are going to be a firecracker in your chosen field and obtain "career confidence."

You need to know your strengths.

If you are going to work effectively, you must know your strengths. You must know what things you do well. There are different levels of strengths.

Novice - You can do something well on a "beginner" level, meaning you can do it, but you may just be learning it.

Intermediate - You can do something "proficiently," which means you do an excellent job at it. However, you are average even though you know all the "nuts and bolts" of the mechanism and how it works (but that is it).

Expert - Last, you have a skill set you have mastered and are considered an "expert." This level is indeed an achievement because you have excelled at the top of the class in this subject matter.

You need to know your weaknesses.

Knowing your weaknesses is almost more critical than knowing your strengths. Nothing will mess you up more than thinking that you are better in an area than you actually are. Owning and acknowledging your weaknesses, both personal and professional, is imperative.

The first step is self-evaluation and reflection. Ask yourself these questions:

- *What areas do I struggle in at work?*
- *What situations have prevented me from doing my best work?*
- *What is the best work environment for my personality and life?*
- *Am I working in a position where I can thrive?*

After evaluating yourself, solicit feedback from a mentor, colleague, or supervisor you trust. Colleagues often provide the most helpful input because they can describe your workflow better than anyone else since you all work together.

Next, if you get quarterly or annual reviews, don't just go through the motions of the assessment. As a manager, I can tell you nothing gets us more excited than someone who owns their issues and is open to feedback. Not all managers are alike, so be wise. If you have a manager who makes you feel seen, heard, and appreciated, that is someone who desires to help you get better.

You need to know the best route to get to your desired destination.

Have you ever been on a road trip? Let me ask another question: have you ever been on a road trip that you *had* to take? For example, you need to go to a city, and you would prefer to fly, but the tickets are out of your price range, so do you have to drive? I have, and nothing is more excruciating than being forced on a road trip you don't want to take. Now, I am not talking about a leisurely, scenic route drive. No, I am talking about reaching your destination, and driving is the **only** solution. In those circumstances, the last thing you want is the longest way. You want to get there as quickly and safely as possible. So, you go to the GPS on your phone and select a route. Now, there is typically more than one option. When multiple choices pop up, they are usually labeled by the ***fastest*** route, the ***suggested*** route, and one long unnamed route that typically avoids the highways. These options occur when a location has multiple ways to get there. For the sake of this discussion, we will only discuss two of the three options: the fastest and suggested routes.

As a manager, I have seen people move up the ladder quickly. At the time of their ascension, everything is going great. However, depending on the individual and the position, they fizzle out fast. Let's go back to our firecracker example. Think about the firework that goes up fast: you think it will be a beautiful display of lights, but it has a quick burst and fizzles out quickly. Well, that can happen to you if you try to reach your desired destination too quickly. I suggest a better route so you can be the firecracker giving minutes of wonder, not seconds.

1. **Professional development** – First, I want you to commit to continuing education. This decision does not mean that you have to go into debt taking out student loans. You can take classes for free online. One of the sites that I like is Coursera, but Khan Academy and EDX are also great options. EDX offers free courses from Harvard University, MIT, and others.

2. **Research the role** – Next, you should research the position you want and the education and skills needed to obtain it. Also, because "success leaves clues," I would go to LinkedIn and study people sitting in your desired seat. Look at the types of jobs that they had along the way. Often, you will see patterns while reviewing the career paths of these individuals.

3. **Mentorship/Career Counseling** – Working with a mentor or career coach can help determine the best route to get to your desired job. Also, you should reach out to a trusted advisor or find a

career coach in your area and work with them on goal-setting exercises to help you achieve your career dreams. An important thing to consider is how long you should stay in each position. Additionally, mentors and coaches can also provide guidance on how to maneuver vertically within the same company. Some companies offer advancement that would also meet your goals. Also, they can help you come up with a plan that meets your goals and your personal priorities. Your top priorities need to be incorporated into your career path. Don't forget to ask yourself tough questions: is financial stability the most important thing to you? Do you crave opportunities to be creative or ones that will stretch outside your comfort zone? How important is work-life balance for you? The answers to these questions should be factored into your overall plan.

If you are reading this book and you are more concerned about creating impact and influence than income, don't worry. The last part of this book is for you. For many, a paycheck is not enough. If that is the case for you, I want you to approach your career goals differently.

Job Influence, Autonomy, & Freedom

Find a job where you can have influence. Some smaller organizations grant more opportunities for autonomy, freedom, and idea execution. If this is important to you, a Fortune 500 company may not be a good fit for you. Bigger organizations, by necessity, must have more policies and procedures. There is much less scope for individual creativity and autonomy. If this matters to you, being part of a sizeable rules-based organization will likely be frustrating.

Personal/Organizational Mission Alignment

If you want to work for a purpose you care deeply about, the public sector and not-for-profit organizations may be a good fit for you. Many choose to work in this sector even though the pay may be significantly less than in mainstream corporations. Ultimately, the affinity and contribution they make to something they deeply care about override the material gains of working in another sector.

The People Factor

If you want to work with people who motivate and inspire you, take some time and research a company's staff and executive leadership team before joining.

Culture & Working with People Who Motivate You

There is no guarantee, but if the individuals that work at an organization have similar interests and backgrounds, there is a higher probability that you will enjoy working with them. Now, personality also has a big part in whether your team is enjoyable. Culture, too, cannot be overlooked when you crave a "specific workplace experience." For example, I desire to work in a place that acknowledges "family" and not an organization where family is an afterthought. I have worked in both environments, and there is no amount of money that I would accept to work for a company that would call me while I am attending a funeral (yes, I know people this has happened to) or out on approved vacation leave. I give one hundred percent at work, so I need that time to be respected when I am out.

At the end of the day, if you are going to possess career confidence and be a firecracker of brilliant light displays, you will have to define, plan, and execute your desired career path or pivot.

CHAPTER 4
SECURING THE BAG: CULTIVATING YOUR BUSINESS

KEY #4 – THE CAMPFIRE SPARK

> camp·fire | ˈkampˌfī(ə)r | noun an open-air fire in a camp, used for cooking and as a focal point for social activity.

Commerce Confidence

Thirty-one million people in the United States are entrepreneurs. Additionally, according to the SBA (Small Business Association), small businesses have generated **12.9 million** net new jobs over the past twenty-five years, accounting for two out of every three jobs added to the economy. Worldwide, there are reported to be 582 million entrepreneurs. Approximately fifty-five percent of adults in the United States have owned a small business. All of these statistics are vital because most of these companies create jobs. This observation is significant because it makes what I call a "campfire spark." Not only does the business warm you, but it can also warm and benefit others. Please do not think I am forcing you to start your own business. There seems to be a massive push on social media to make everyone go out and create an LLC. Being an entrepreneur is not for the faint of heart.

Gregg Throgmartin, CEO of *Skin Laundry*, defines the term *entrepreneur* this way:

"...an entrepreneur is someone who can paint a vision of something that has never before existed, then work tirelessly to make it happen. Someone who lives and breathes their business, not because they have to, but because they love to. An entrepreneur is curious, passionate, and not afraid to dive headfirst into an area of opportunity where almost everyone else has failed before. They can either tune out the large chorus saying, "This won't work," or get fired up by the challenge to uncover and prove out just how it can work."

Does any part of this description describe you? If so, this is the easiest time in history to start your business; whether you are creating a side hustle to increase your income or establish a company—you need commerce confidence to bring your vision to pass. And it would be great to embrace this confidence key while you build your empire. After you have created it, you will have new lists of wins and woes to celebrate and endure. There are four aspects I want you to understand about launching, relaunching, or excelling in your business endeavors.

Step One: Decide

It all starts with a decision. After you affirm within yourself that you are ready to take the plunge, get a solid plan. Create a clear business plan that will be the foundation of your entrepreneurial success. Take the time to consider your business's mission, objectives, and strategies. One critical decision that comes up pretty quickly is your business name.

Contrary to popular belief, you cannot select any name you want. Check your name popularity and availability on your Secretary of State's website and the U.S. Patent and Trademark Office. Also, do web searches to ensure that your potential name has not been used negatively or criminally in any way. Here are some additional considerations:

Business Name Selection

First, you must select a Business Name. There are a lot of factors when choosing a name, but here are a few to consider:

- **Keep it short and simple**—your name will drive all your marketing materials, so not necessarily short, but precise will always be best. Also, remember that your website domain, social media channels, and other promotional items will contain your business name.
- **Think global**—in our global economy, please keep your business name in mind as it will translate into other languages.

Once selected, you should take precautions to secure your business name. Here are the measures of protection for your chosen business name.

Business Name Protection

- **Federal:** Register a federal trademark with U.S. Patent and Trademark Office
- **State:** Form a corporation, LLC, or register a state trademark
- **County:** File an assumed name certificate at your county clerk's office
- **Digital:** Reserve your website domain and social media accounts

Step Two: Declare

Talk the talk, and walk the walk of your business. Begin to build your personal and business brands. This mantra will require that you write your vision and make it plain. Writing it down will also aid in your overall organization. Your systems are essential to help you stay on track and complete tasks on time.

Step Three: Demonstrate

Show you are prepared through your research, marketing plans, legal precautions, and accounting set-up. Once these steps are complete, you are ready to do business when you have done these things. Your research includes learning about the competition and the industry in which you plan to do business. This process also includes selecting the ideal business location, which can significantly impact its success. Reviewing zoning laws, checking out the local economy, and doing the groundwork (probing surrounding areas to find the perfect spot for your business) are also necessities. Next, you should develop a comprehensive marketing strategy to help get your business in front of potential customers. This strategy incorporates who you have identified as your audience, what they need, and have an answer for their problem/pain points. Finally, ensure that your business is set up correctly. Your business should comply with all local, state, and federal laws. Hire a qualified accountant to help you with financial management and tax reporting. When starting, you must separate your business and personal funds. Look up the best banks and credit unions in your area for small businesses. Then establish a primary account (income) with sub-accounts for operating expenses, payroll, and taxes. I suggest you start with a payroll account even if you are a sole proprietor because it is easy to pay yourself correctly if you start out doing so. It is hard to break bad business habits. Your accountant can explain more about selecting the correct business entity. The most common are sole proprietorships, limited liability companies (LLCs), and corporations. Once your business becomes profitable, your goal will be to reduce your tax liability. When this occurs, ask your accountant about an S-Corp classification. They can explain it to you in detail and help you decide if and when this is a good fit for your business.

Step Four: Deliver

Be ready to show up, do the work, ship the goods, coach the clients, and make your customers' lives better. As your business needs change, you may have to hire or outsource tasks to maintain or enhance your product or service. I highly recommend a business coach or mentor (in your price range) that can help you achieve continued success.

The Importance of Creating a Meaningful Brand

One last point is the importance of branding. I mentioned briefly above that your digital presence is enormous in this virtual era. My good friend and colleague Rainah Davis discusses this in her book, *Activate: Building a Purposeful and Profitable Brand in a Tribe-Based Culture (2019)*. I have permission to share some key elements from her valuable resource. Creating a meaningful brand that is humanized (with your personality) requires four components:

1. Define your Brand (Give it interest)
2. Give it Friends, Companions (Discover your friends, best audience)
3. Development a Content Plan (Blog, email, audio/video strategy, social media)
4. Design your brand (Give it a face, dress, identity)

Defining your brand and giving it friends is about the audience: the people you are uniquely qualified to serve and, more importantly, that you want to help. Successful online marketers often share similar content, but the differentiator is unique to their background and their story. Two marketers who do this well are Marie Forleo and Nicole Walters. Both influencers emphasized that their paths to success were achieved by clearly identifying **who** they wanted to support and help. Both businesswomen also express that the surest way to fail was by focusing on the money they wanted to make instead of the individual who would benefit from their product or service.

Now, let's be clear, we all need income. However, our business can't just only be about profit. We all need to be able to pay our bills, but if you are only building a brand to produce profit, you have already set yourself up to fail. The key is to focus on making a difference. In Dany Ivy's book, *Audience Revolution,* he shares some valuable gems on this subject matter. First, he begins by saying that you make a difference by establishing a connection with your audience. This connection is about gradually increased intimacy.

Remember when you started dating your significant other? It would have been weird to walk up to them, tell them that you have been watching them, that you think they are *the one*, and that you would like to introduce them to your parents. In that case, any average person would see you as a bit of psycho and most likely get away from you as quickly as possible. Well, connecting with an audience has similar steps to building most healthy relationships. It starts with a shared interest and how you make the other person "feel." If you bring them joy, answer a problem, or help them see life more clearly, they are more likely to want to keep you around. That is how it starts in the business world as well.

You share content with your audience (for free) because you want to help. You are uniquely qualified to help your viewers avoid pitfalls or struggles you have faced and overcome. Although she is no longer with us, Instagram influencer Cici Gunn (also known as @theSixFigureChick) always dropped gems on this subject matter. She stated that free information should be the "what" information, while "how to do it" should be your paid content. The highest elevation of your purpose is being able to solve problems for people at a profit. There is truly no greater joy than getting paid for something that you love to do.

Ivy shares Gunn's sentiments. You must take your audience into paid content because, as Ivy declares: "cost and commitment go together." There is only so much value associated with your free content; your goal should be giving people enough free information to recognize the value of your time/product/service and establish that you have something to offer that is worth an investment. More importantly, it helps people take you and your product seriously. With this information in mind, you should be ready to select or redefine your business model.

The *Activate* book shares these **four business models**:

1. Product-based (People who sell products)
2. Service-based (People who provide services)
3. Content-driven (People who write/publish/create content/blog)
4. Voice-driven (People who speak/provide training/create podcasts & videos)
5. Informational Track: inform or educate on one or more related areas

6. Inspirational Track: share inspiration/motivation in one or more areas

So, after you have worked hard to put your audience first, create a difference, and provide quality content through one of these four business models, the next step is to build your business model through the lens of servant leadership. Servant leadership unlocks a life cycle that leads you to create a significant impact by changing the lives of those within your audience. Next, it opens the sweet spot of empathy and intimacy, leading to connection, care, and in-depth transformation.

By focusing on the activities, you love and providing high inspiration, you create abundance, which increases your income by allowing you to charge premium rates. The cumulation of all these activities leads to the creation of lasting relationships and business longevity. This chapter is by no means everything you need to know to start your business. However, I hope you will be motivated to begin your journey or continue.

Go Light Your Campfire Spark

Lastly, this section is considered the campfire spark because business provides opportunities for your light and fire to benefit others. I want to make one thing abundantly clear. I am writing this chapter for individuals who still work their 9a-5p or 4p-11p, or 12a-8p shift jobs and those who are full-time business owners. I am not telling anyone they must rush off and quit their job. I believe the best time to build a business is when you do not have to depend entirely on that business income to eat.

I believe that side hustles are the new job security. These businesses unlock the doors to financial freedom quicker than almost any other path. Financial freedom looks very different for every person, so some of the ways that I define it are:

- The freedom to design your schedule.
- The freedom to walk away from a job that mistreats you.
- The freedom to create extra income.
- The freedom to pay yourself what you are worth.
- The freedom to retire earlier.

These freedoms create increased opportunities, such as:
- extra funds for a vacation
- income for additional help (such as nannies, house cleaners, or landscapers)
- money to assist in eliminating looming debts such as medical bills, credit card debt, and student loans

Your commerce confidence will bless those who use your products and obtain your services. Also, the people that you hire will benefit from the source of income that you will provide. This period is the easiest time to create wealth through this path. Please don't hesitate to ignite your campfire spark and walk in your commerce confidence.

Disclaimer: I am not an accountant or business advisor. This chapter is based on my own research and experience. Please do your own due diligence to ensure that you set up your business based on your own individual needs and goals.

CHAPTER 5
CREATING FINANCIAL SECURITY & A LEGACY OF WEALTH

KEY#5 – THE TORCH SPARK

torch | tôrCH | noun *mainly historical,* a portable means of illumination such as a piece of wood or cloth soaked in tallow or an oil lamp on a pole, sometimes carried ceremonially | (usually **the torch**) used to refer to a valuable quality, principle, or cause that needs to be protected and maintained.

Compound Coin Confidence

Before the Olympic Games opening, there is a torch-lighting ceremony. This ancient ritual is still in existence today. I want to propose that we begin to see legacy in that same way. Instead of defining financial security as only having a large savings account, a healthy investment portfolio, and a comfortable retirement nest egg, I endeavor to help you obtain financial freedom and legacy. In actuality, proper financial protection is about much more than just money. It's also about feeling in control of your life and having the freedom to choose how to live it. Compound coin confidence happens when you focus on legacy and plan for it regardless of your current circumstances. There are a few things to keep in mind as we dive into this chapter.

Commitment

Before we get started, I want to drive home the first step into igniting the torch spark that gives you and your heirs compound coin confidence. The first vital step is commitment. If you are going to do this, it will require sacrifice, and if you are a first-generation legacy builder, it will require seeking financial education. We live in the easiest era to make money. Side hustle culture is widely accepted and even expected in some regions. Any accountant will tell you that it is not how much money you *make* but how much money you *keep* that is key! I want you to take that leap and decide that you are going to take dominion in this legacy arena. Legacy is more than leaving something behind—it's like life insurance, even though life insurance is a critical way to secure an inheritance.

Inheritance is a vital element of generational wealth. Generational wealth, also known as a family legacy or wealth, gets transferred from generation to generation. It can occur after the death of a parent or another family member or during a person's life. Wealth is passed down from one generation to the next. You can leave something behind for your children or grandchildren. In that case, you are contributing to the growth of generational wealth in your family. Of course, you may leave many things, such as good memories and healthy genetics, behind for your family. However, generational wealth deals with the financial resources your loved ones can inherit.

Wealth legacy occurs when general wealth is passed down within a family to multiple generations. The first generation accumulates revenue and property during their lifetime, which they then pass down to their children. With successful and proper planning, those children can then pass down wealth to their children, and so on. Generational wealth can be in the form of cash, savings, property, life insurance, investments, bitcoin, crypto, and other forms of NFTs. It can also consist of family-owned businesses or valuable possessions such as artwork, antiques, and jewelry.

Committing to Building Generational Wealth

Again, I applaud your decision if you are starting from scratch with your finances and attempting to be a first-generation wealth builder. You are setting future generations of your lineage up for success. How different would your life be if your parents could have been able to fund your college education? Instead, if you are in the majority, you are playing catch up to pay down your student loan debt. You could have saved for your first home or future retirement without that indebtedness. Additionally, without loads of debt, your financial future is more stable.

By preparing for your child's future today, you can help them get a running start on their finances. That's what it means to build generational wealth. It creates a solid foundation for your child's economic success, which they can continue to build upon for future generations. The benefits of generational wealth bring financial security to the family. The next generation that follows will have far less debt because wealth exists for them. Also, they are empowered with the means to increase their earnings by starting businesses without having to secure predatory loans or high-interest credit cards. For future generations, they can use their assets to grow their wealth and leave money and property to their family when they pass to be financially comfortable; then, they can invest and grow these assets for the next generation.

Generational wealth also benefits communities and the country in some cases. The remaining family may decide to invest in a new business or grow an existing business. Small family-run businesses are the cornerstones of many communities. They employ other people to run the business, giving them and their families more financial security. When they spend their money, they boost the country's economic growth.

An inheritance can offer much-needed resources when one is also just starting their adult life. It can teach your children or grandchildren how to be independent and resourceful. A financial boost at the right time can also help remove some of the pressure that stunts innovation and distracts them from pursuing their dreams.

Once wealth is accumulated, it is essential to establish wills and trusts to distribute assets wisely. Another benefit is that inheritance trusts can drive success. Instead of providing an inheritance outright, parents and grandparents can use the funds to create an incentive by establishing trusts through their financial advisors or estate planning specialists. This strategy allows them to choose the conditions under which their assets are passed onto the next generation. For example, heirs may be required to complete a degree program to receive a lump sum or use the trust only for specified purposes, such as to start a business. Individuals can then shape how the assets they leave behind actively benefit those who receive them. Here are a few components of wills and trusts:

1. Wills and trusts are effective tools to ensure that your assets and property are distributed according to your wishes after your death.
2. A will is a legally binding document that outlines how your assets will be distributed, who will serve as your executor and guardian for your children, and other wishes.
3. A trust is a legal agreement where a person (the grantor) transfers the ownership of their assets or property to another person (the trustee) to manage and distribute according to the grantor's wishes.
4. Wills and trusts can be used to minimize taxes and protect assets from creditors.
5. Wills and trusts should be reviewed regularly as laws and family circumstances change over time. Generational wealth isn't a once-off inheritance that you spend in your lifetime. Instead, it is wealth

that is structured to last forever from generation to generation. Generational wealth is about making your money work for you and your family across generations. I have often heard, "If you don't come from a wealthy family, a wealthy family can come from you." It just takes one person to commit to starting the process. If you are blessed enough to be a part of a family that has begun this process, please don't drop the baton. Build on the inheritance already established and teach your children to follow suit.

Choosing an Investment Strategy

There are two investment paths that can fund your generational wealth. One path is stock investment, and the second is real estate.

Path 1: Stock Investment

Investing in stocks means buying tiny shares of ownership in a public company. Those small shares are known as the company's stock, and by investing in them, you're hoping the company grows and performs well over time. If that happens, your shares may become more valuable, and other investors may be willing to buy them from you for more than you paid. That means you could earn a profit if you decide to sell them.

Six Steps of Stock Investment:

- Decide how you want to invest in the stock market
- Choose an investing account
- Learn the difference between investing in stocks and funds
- Set a budget for your stock market investment
- Focus on investing for the long-term
- Manage your stock portfolio

Investment Selection Factors

The answer to what you choose to invest in comes down to two things: the time horizon for your goals and how much risk you're willing to take. Let's tackle the time horizon first: if you're investing for a far-off objective like retirement, you should invest primarily in stocks. Investing in stocks will allow your money to grow and outpace inflation. As your goal gets closer, you can slowly dial back your stock allocation and add more bonds—generally safer investments.

Finally, the other factor is risk tolerance. The stock market goes up and down. If you're prone to panicking when it does the latter, you're better off investing slightly more conservatively, with a lighter allocation to stocks.

Path 2: Real Estate Investment

Real estate is an incredibly unique asset class with various underlying characteristics and strategies that can serve multiple purposes for an investor. Here are a few of its multifaceted advantages to understand the attraction to this particular asset.

Passive Income – Passive real estate investments don't require a full-time commitment. They also allow investors to leverage their capital across multiple assets to generate multiple income streams instead of sinking all their assets into a single purchase.

Easily Transferable – Real estate is easily transferable to succeeding generations. The affluent typically set up trusts to hold their real estate assets, and upon the grantor's passing away, ownership automatically transfers through the trust. Real estate conveyances at death are much less complicated than conveyances of business disagreements that may arise in roles, compensation, contributions, distributions, etc.

I am not a financial strategist or advisor. The information provided is based on my own research. Please do your due diligence to initiate and fund your legacy. Now that I have explained what generational wealth is and some paths to fund it, I want to help you eliminate the mindset that hinders you from igniting your touch spark and achieving compound coin confidence.

Breaking the Chains of the Poverty Mindset

To ensure a better perspective for yourself, you must be willing to dispose of faulty thinking. For example, at one point in my life, I worked two full-time jobs for three years straight to provide for my family. Whenever I shared this experience with others, most people responded that they could never endure that. I usually answered them silently because I agreed with them; God gave *me* that assignment because He knew I could handle it. However, had I been consumed with negative thoughts, there is a chance I could've missed out on the opportunity to take care of my loved ones.

Though things worked out for me, negative mentalities commonly enslave others. For some, the fear of waste is so severe that they are willing to live significantly below their means to preserve their income. This concept is otherwise known as a "poverty mindset." To further illustrate, I'd like to introduce a quote I once heard. It went like this, "Poor people will use a bar of soap until it looks like a SIM card." This saying infers that lower-level thinking is a form of protection for the less fortunate: they attempt to preserve the little they have by using even less.

Though we never know when we may fall on hard times, we must enjoy the fruits of our labor in seasons of prosperity. If you live with a poverty mindset, you risk losing the gift that God has granted you. This reminds me of another quote: **"You'll never make it to your destination if you stop at the rocks that every dog barks at**." Your mentality will adjust if you listen to every negative voice you hear. Instead, choose discernment. Suppose you can learn to discern which situations require a reasonable amount of money. In that case, you will be able to better invest in yourself.

Answering the Legacy Call

After you have analyzed your level of poverty mindset, you should prepare yourself for God's calling. For example, one of the themes we find in the Bible is identity and self-confidence. When God called Moses, he said, "Who am I?" Although this man was unsure of his identity, he trusted God to reveal his purpose in due time.

Can you relate to Moses' situation? Are you someone with a calling on their life who is overwhelmed with a lack of confidence? As Scripture exemplifies, you should remember to use what you have. Even though Moses had a rod and a speech impediment, God told him to *go*; go and open his mouth. Since Moses chose to be obedient, the Lord provided everything he needed.

We can learn a lot from Moses' obedience. Such as, God doesn't need our *ability*—He needs our *availability*. Remember, God is all-powerful. We can do all things through Christ who strengthens us (Philippians 4:13) because He can do exceedingly, abundantly, above all that we ask for (Ephesians 3:20). Therefore, if you're waiting on God to respond to your prayer, you should also prepare to answer His call.

Don't miss out on your God-given opportunity because of poor planning. One reason new businesses, ministries, or relationships aren't established is that the individuals involved lack confidence. For instance, what if Jeff Bezos never had the testicular fortitude to start an online bookstore in his garage? Then he never would've become the multi-millionaire he is today.

To clarify, the Bible does not say God will *give* you wealth; instead, the Bible gives you the power to *get* wealth. Take Dr. Drè's visionary Beats headphones, for example. At one point, his musical partner Eminem attempted to dissuade him from working on Beats so they could focus on new music. Despite his feedback, Drè continued to produce Beats and eventually took over the industry for listening devices. It wasn't long after this that the musical genius sold Beats to Apple for one billion dollars.

Ultimately, Drè had a billion-dollar business idea but could've easily gotten distracted from his purpose. The vision was already in his head, but he had to *answer the call* to activate it. Without confidence, Drè may have made another hit album, sold a couple of records, and ignored his innovative dream. It's safe to say that, in hindsight, he is grateful he made the right decision to proceed with his invention.

Now it's time for you to reflect. Do you have a million-dollar patent in mind that you fear acting on? If so, I hope these stories have inspired you to implement your plan. I challenge you this week to take the next step and answer God's calling. The supernatural calling within you will give you the fortitude to be the game-changer or maintainer of your family legacy. I challenge and encourage you to be the torchbearer of your generation.

CONCLUSION

As you conclude this reading, I hope you realize you have the sparks within you to walk with confidence and win in every area of life. This conclusion aims to give you a summary of the tools you need to embrace every spark outlined in the previous chapters. Remember this: **you are not the average person**. There is no better time than now to level up.

Attaching your identity to your performance may seem scary at first. Still, it is an excellent way to hold yourself accountable. This is because you know what you are capable of and should not accept anything less than your best. It is also important to note that **going to the next level means going from being a master to being a rookie**. During this transition, trust in God to help you accomplish your destiny.

It's okay if you feel uncomfortable maintaining a growth mindset and learning new things. Don't be afraid to risk your comfort zone to prepare for your higher calling. If you ever feel fatigued, rest from your aspirations, recalibrate and refuel—but never quit. See that you continue on the path that leads to your success.

Competence Leads to Confidence

When you work for next-level confidence, you develop an inherent peace. However, if success comes too fast, often, you won't be able to maintain it. Taking the time to grow slowly will allow you to release foolish thinking and gain wisdom that will benefit you in the long run.

For example, years ago, I learned that no one in my family had ever been broadcasted on a network. No one in my family ever sat down with networks or production assistants to secure a position on television, even though they sought various roles on media channels. I was also unfamiliar with the details, but my confidence encouraged me to learn more about the process. I never feared the outcome or whether my attempts would be fruitful. I wanted information, and eventually, I received the answers I was seeking.

To develop competence, you must surround yourself with knowledgeable people and enrich yourself with skills. Take heed to wise advice and research ways to solve problems. Watch as your resilience, power, and internal drive increase your pursuit of excellence. Consider this, the best basketball players obtained their success by taking their first shot. Before that, the players developed solid bonds and trusted their teammates to perform on the court. They had to have the proper training to outweigh their opponents. Ultimately, their accumulation of knowledge and skills led to extreme self-assurance.

Assets & Liabilities

As you succeed on your confidence journey, note the assets and liabilities you may accrue along the way. You can be a shining example and mentor to others if you prioritize your spending and manage your wealth well. However, you can't teach young people how to develop confidence and accomplish their goals if you are mishandling your talents. Instead, learn to leave behind a legacy—not accrued debt.

Although the pressure to look rich is tempting, refrain from submitting to the hype. Trying to *keep up with the Joneses* is not profitable; this endless pursuit will add to your liabilities and reduce your assets. So, does making expensive purchases and being irresponsible with your income mean you lack confidence? Possibly. Ask yourself this: **what does that say about my priorities? Is there any scenario where a lack of confidence would drive me to want to *look* rich rather than *be* rich?**

If you answered "Yes," to that question, consider how often we see Warren Buffet or Jeff Bezos walking around with $10,000 worth of jewelry. The answer may surprise you. These multi-millionaires don't typically flaunt their wealth materialistically. On the contrary, they have confidence-related drives and aren't attention seekers; we can learn much from their humility.

In addition to financial factors, some cognitive assets and liabilities affect our confidence levels. For instance, perhaps you endured a cycle of trauma as a child. As you grow and mature in your identity, will you carry those burdens with you? Into your personal relationships? Into your business(es)? Into your home? I certainly hope not. Alternatively, you can change the narrative by going against the generational curses you may be up against. Be willing to stand against substance abuse, gambling, theft, and/or sexual immorality if needed; free yourself from the temptations that easily entice you. Once you do, you will recognize that your dedication will overflow into all areas of your life.

Need Help Igniting Your Spark?

If you have gotten to the end of this book and feel as though you want to obtain the five keys, but need help, fret not. You do not have to walk this path alone.

I have a free Spark Coaching & Academy assessment for you. Please go www.Ignitemysparks.com to get started.

If you got what you needed and are ready to go, I am so excited. Please tell me about your journey and how it's going by connecting with me on social. I can't wait to hear your stories!

- 📷 : @Tyrusjhinton2
- 🐦 : @Tyrusjhinton
- 📘 : @Tyrusjhinton
- 🎵 : @Tyrusjhinton

www.ingramcontent.com/pod-product-compliance
Lightning Source LLC
Chambersburg PA
CBHW070431010526
44118CB00014B/2001